Dancing in the Rain

Dancing in the Rain

Chris Moran

To John
for his unconditional love and support and, of course,
the carrot/hazelnut loaves!

Bennison Books
A good book is a blessing

Copyright ©2015 Bennison Books
Copyright Chris Moran
All rights reserved
First published 2015

This book is sold subject to the condition that it shall not be reproduced in any form without the prior written permission of the author and Bennison Books. Brief quotations may be used without permission in articles or reviews.

Cover illustration by Diane M. Denton

Bennison Books Poetic Licence
ISBN: 978-1507602102

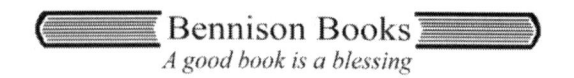

Bennison Books
A good book is a blessing

Contents

Introduction 1
About the Author 3
Breaking Free 5
Part One: Leaning with Cézanne 7

    Apology 9
    Winter 10
    Still Time 11
    Falling Leaves 12
    Cyclamen 13
    Escape 14
    Summer Prayer 16
    This Day 17
    Spider 18
    Being Nothing 19
    Bees 20
    Something of God 21
    Leaning with Cézanne 22
    Villanelle 24

Part Two: The Years Were Minutes 25

    Reprieve 27
    The Summer of '67 29
    Our Mother 31
    Elephant Trousers 32
    Mothering 33
    One-Way Ticket 34
    To Remember You 36
    Caesarean Section 37
    Mirror 39

Birthday Meal 40
At the Hairdresser's 41
God's Wonderful World 42
Smiling at Death 43
Transposition 45
Suitcase 46
Baby Haiku 48
I'm the One 49
What It Is 50
This is Holiday 51
Awestruck 52
For Theodore, aged 3 53
Innocence 54
Solomon's Light 55
Song of Life 56

Part Three: Drowning 57

Daughter 59
Phoebe and Me 60
Surrender 61
Painting the Future 62
Sobriety – Ten Years On 63

Part Four: Dancing in the Rain 65

MRI Scan 67
Lost in the Post 69
What It's About 70
A Bad Good Dream 71
The Party's Over 72
Teacher 73
Real 74
Incredulous 75
Trapped 76
Shoes 77

What I Thought Was Mine	78
Dancing in the Dark	79
Wilmer	80
Accepting Acceptance	81
My Body	82
Caramelised Hazelnut Praline	83
Neutral	84
It's Okay	85
A Dog's Perspective	86
Please Don't Cry	87
Truth	88
Letting Go of the Knife	89
Coming in from the Cold	90
Falling Skyward	91
Dancing in the Rain	92
If It Works	93
Fear	94
Still	95
Morning Prayer	96
Now	97
All This	98
Don't Let Go	99
Be Awake	101

What day is it? asked Winnie-the-Pooh
It's today, squeaked Piglet
My favourite day, said Pooh
A.A. Milne

Live the actual moment. Only this moment is life.
Thich Nhat Hahn

Introduction
By Diane M. Denton

I met Chris Moran at the beginning of her journey through poetry. I heard her: quiet, even uncertain, but not cautious. She was speaking of being diagnosed with multiple sclerosis (MS), how she felt suffocated and strangled by it, and, yet, was wondering if she might starve its appetite for power over her. I was introduced to her as she unexpectedly found herself following the music of words as poets do, and discovering how to use her voice as singers do. I encountered her past and present and future, her joys and sorrows, what was dear to her heart and as important to her soul, and her humour that defied her struggle like sunshine on a stormy day.

I became her friend as she became mine, immediately, and over time and the miles that, fortunately, modern technology removed, until I was honoured to be asked to create the artwork for the cover of this anthology and write its introduction.

Chris has said the poet in her would never have emerged if it wasn't for MS, which makes me think of how life tricks us – not always in the kindest ways – into doing what we are meant to do. Passions, talents and callings, like obsessive lovers, seek us out and, no matter how we reject them, eventually, inevitably, prove irresistible.

I believe Chris has always been a poet. I suspect that long before she acknowledged her muse it was waiting in the wings, watching the scenes of her life play out, realising her innate awareness, sensitivity, honesty, wit and imagination, and, all the while, hoping – knowing – she would one day turn its way.

It must be a happy muse now. From beginning her blog in 2011 to the publication of this volume, Chris has collaborated with it far beyond her initial motivation of self-therapy. Her poetry lives for its own sake. It's eclectic and entertaining, even whimsical, spiritual and philosophical, deeply personal and relatable. There's gentle power in it, but its expression is never forced. It breezes amongst the flowers and bees, notices the nuances of the seasons, takes a dog's view, plays like a child, animates a wheelchair, and considers the colour of cushions. It looks back with pain, laughter and love, and ahead with trepidation and hope. It handles loss and recovery, juggles resentment and gratitude.

Its simplest offerings are never simplistic, the harshest never unrelenting. Where there is form there is still freedom. Every word, every stanza, every observation, every question, every understanding – all the aspects of Chris's journey through life *and* poetry – reflect her beautiful spirit that, rain or shine, will keep on dancing.

Diane M. Denton is a writer and artist from Buffalo, New York. She has written two works of historical fiction published by All Things That Matter Press: A House Near Luccoli, *and its sequel,* To A Strange Somewhere Fled.

About the Author

A diagnosis of progressive multiple sclerosis three years ago caused the foundations of my comfortable life to tremble. They were not totally shaken, however, as I had known deep inside myself for many years that something was wrong. But doctors, including neurologists, dismissed my symptoms and told me I was anxious and stressed; I wasn't. But if the experts tell you often enough you begin to believe them.

I started having severe panic attacks and eventually discovered that a sip of brandy would bring relief. I was about to travel down a very dark path. Alcoholism waited patiently and eventually gripped me so hard there seemed to be no escape. I reached rock bottom and was very near death when something inside me, which I may never understand, caused me to 'wake up'.

Through the Alcoholics Anonymous programme I have now enjoyed twelve very contented years of sobriety.

I believe there is something waiting inside us all, yearning to be given a chance, and sometimes it seems adversity holds the key. I think this was so for me. If I hadn't succumbed to alcoholism resulting in an eventual spiritual awakening and a long haul back from the depths of despair into the light, I am certain my previous mindset would not have coped healthily with the onset of a serious condition; I would surely have drunk myself to death.

And if not for this diagnosis and an urgent need to express my thoughts and feelings, my creativity may have remained locked in. So very slowly, although my body threatens to fail me, my spirit has been freed and everything is beginning to make sense.

Of course, all this may simply be what I want to believe. But what I do know is that anger has no useful place, although I harboured much for the medical profession for many years for not giving me an early diagnosis.

There comes a time for us all, particularly for those of us who have heard a constant nagging voice in the background whispering, 'I can't', to step up and say, 'Here I am'. For me, that time is now.

Life is too short for it to be filled with anger; it can always be beautiful if we allow it to be. Every moment counts, good and bad, and I want to live them all to the full, not just wade my way through. This is now my time, not only to survive, but to thrive.

Chris Moran, 2015

All profits received by the author from the sale of this book will be donated to The Multiple Sclerosis Trust.

Breaking Free

The trick is to know when,
and for those who truly seek to bloom
their time will come.

There will be an urgency
like a rebirth,
the years of confinement over
and time to take a risk,
to burst through,
break loose from the safety
of the bud and say
Here I am.

This is true discernment,
a risking of good for better
and better for best.
Because a bud will eventually
outgrow its purpose
and if not broken
will droop, hang limp,
a withered head, brittle
and packed tight with
the crushed brown petals
of what could have been.

CM

Part One
Leaning with Cézanne

Apology

Today I see it differently,
the veil lifted.
Apologise for my
previous flimsy interest
and look now, entranced,
at the miracle of it all,
and feel a pointless sadness
that it took so long
for me to see.

Winter

How sad and pale the tree is looking now
her faded skin, dry bones that pierce through
and shiver every twig along the bough
as if she dreads what now may be her due.
Does she grieve the loss of summer's face
when filled with life she whispered with the breeze,
or simply bow her head with gentle grace
to brilliance that waits beneath to please
our aching hearts, for all, it seems, is dead.
There is no rush, the earth will slowly move
her way through darkness, new seeds to be fed
and once again her certainty will prove
that season's change has come for reasons known,
embryonic life already sown.

Still Time

Today has a different feel,

it's warm enough to open the doors.

I watch the sun

play a game with spring

though I think this is just winter

on a coffee break.

Are the green shoots being fooled

or am I?

They poke through the soil and grass,

talk about new beginnings,

how life can start over and still shine.

Maybe it's not too late for me;

perhaps there is still time.

Falling Leaves

Tinged with weariness of defeat
they cling to a life that's done
and wait.
Scudding clouds pass
swift with purpose.

The leaves fall
and as their melancholy
greets the earth they rest.
But only for a while

for they too

still have

purpose.

Cyclamen

You look imprisoned
in your small plastic pot,
as though you could burst.
You have so much to offer,
yet there you sit
Reduced to Clear
in big red letters,
waiting for reprieve,
a chance to show your worth.

I wonder if anyone will see you,
I mean really see
your eager roots
in their dark padded cell
of organised chaos,
a quilted bed of heartthrob leaves
urging slender stems to reach
toward papery petalled awareness.

We all blossom in our own time;
in our own way.
Neither you nor I
have anything to prove.

Escape

Laid bare upon the grass
this tiny thing,
already viewed as prey
though not yet equipped
for fight or flight,
too much demanded too soon
of a newly formed heart
still rehearsing its beat.

I form a cradle,
a makeshift nest
in the palm of my hand
where it sits motionless,
and stunned.
How can anything this small
be so complete?
I feel privileged for the
closeness of the moment,
this timeless piece of time,
caress the silky back of
minuscule speckles,
underbelly a mass of fluffy down,
this frantic pulse of new life
determined not to quit.
A powerful silence
as we both wait;
I could burst with love.

Minutes pass;

fear finally abates,
a cue to unfold my hand.
A nearby buddleia bush
sways in the evening breeze,
protective arms open wide,
a bivouac of branches
for a small handful of life
waiting to soar.
The world is a big place.

Summer Prayer

There's so much commotion
in the garden today,
nature's busy town square;
eager bees deep in petunia hearts,
moments of shared passion,
summer's lust.
Ornamental grasses wave,
coaxed into Chinese whispers
by a playful breeze,
butterflies dizzy with
fluttery-giggle-fits.
A red admiral is stunned;
it's all too much for her,
fragile wings quiver, exhausted.
She stops, completely used up.
I fear she must be dead,
approach her gently, tearful,
holding a sorrowful summer prayer.
But she startles me,
opens her rested wings,
takes hold of the prayer and
flies off into forget-me-not blue.
Perhaps she will save it
for a rainy day.

This Day

The feeling you can't explain
when everything seems just right
and nothing could be wrong,
even though you have a list
as long as your arm
of things you want to change.

But not on this day
when the bee dives headlong
into an unknown depth,
stays for unconscionable time,
then emerges intoxicated,
head to toe in smudges,
powdery white – hint of blush.

And when birds sing from the
very tops of swaying trees,
because praise calls out to be sung
from the highest point.
So where else would they go?
I know only too well that
it will end,
not in a blaze of glory way,
but softly handing itself over
to a comforting, slowly darkening,
in-between space.

Spider

The trees whisper me
into their awareness.
I choose one to sit beneath
breathing in their comfort,
sharing their world
on a day to remember
when I finally see us all as one.
A tiny spider walks across my hand,
stops halfway for a rest,
then carries on.

Being Nothing

To sit beneath the tree
in my garden
doing nothing
being nothing
just for a few moments
is the one thing
I can be sure of
to take me right back
to the beginning,
to strip everything away
and start again
with compassion
and a grateful heart

Bees

My deep and passionate love affair with bees
blossomed in the lavender bed last year.
I never thought it possible for me
that I could hold such tiny things so dear;
the way they burrow deep inside a flower,
and weave their song among the pollen dust.
I sit and watch for hour upon hour
and know that if I'm still I have their trust.
I gaze upon transparent little wings
designed by whom, or did they just evolve?
It seems to be a mystery that clings
to all of us, a chance that we may solve
or maybe not, and would it seem so odd
to think that all of this is down to God?

Something of God

seems to flow through me
when I see fruits of dandelion
fly off to follow seedling dreams,
when mischievous clouds
daub wild horses and hearts
on a cerulean work of art
or a large bird lands
with unshakeable faith
on slender branch.
When I feel warm water
flow smooth over thirsty hands,
touch virgin pages of a book
as fresh folds of indigo night
wrap me in hope
but leave me almost afraid to sleep
in case I lose it,
in case the blackness wipes it all away
leaving morning's aching doubt.
And then just after sunrise
I see a small tortoiseshell butterfly
land softly on the sedum.

God is a circle whose centre is everywhere and circumference nowhere ~ Voltaire

Leaning with Cézanne

The garden is a timeless world
with no map;
I simply lean a little more
to the right or left
as did Cézanne
and see it all.
I sit among the flowers
alone but not lonely;
they have become friends,
the kind who stay around,
forgive and maybe even forget,
keep with you
when fear grips and
nothing makes sense.
Bees forage without regrets;

I can only move forward,
thoughts now infused with gratitude
for the privilege of life.
They become soft,
muted with warmth,
welcome antithesis of
yesterday's sharp edges.
Elated birdsong
disperses the stillness and
although I have no idea
who or what is holding me together
I feel safe,
for today at least,

and that is enough.

Here on the river's verge, I could be busy for months without changing my place, simply leaning a little more to the right or left. ~ Paul Cézanne

Villanelle

The pale pink loveliness of spring awaits
To shower blushes, bring the earth alive
Her beauty will unfold to eyes that wake

But keep them closed and you will be too late
Like buds unopened never to arrive
The pale pink loveliness of spring awaits

The lowly petalled snowdrops will collate
Firm promises to thrive, not just survive
Her beauty will unfold to eyes that wake

And as the bitter winter chill abates
And earth's cold heart is aching to revive
The pale pink loveliness of spring awaits

Then will the welcome birdsong be elate
And rainbow arcs of colour boldly strive
Her beauty will unfold to eyes that wake

So do not linger, let your soul lustrate
In spring's cool waters like a swallow dive
The pale pink loveliness of spring awaits
Her beauty will unfold to eyes that wake

Part Two
The Years Were Minutes

Reprieve

Chapel was compulsory
in our household,
unless you were nearly dead,
which was how I often felt
after Saturday night
at the youth club.
Or to be more precise,
The Red Lion Pub.

If you don't come then
you'll peel all the vegetables
for dinner

God didn't approve of jeans either
unless you were Catholic,
then he didn't mind one way or another.
But we were Methodist to the core;
a weekly dose of pleated obedience -
below the knee.

Arrows of hellfire and damnation
fired from the pulpit
aimed solely at me
because I was the one
who didn't want to be there
and God knew it;
I was marked down in his
book of badness every week.
But even if God hated me

attendance was rewarded;
one more reprieve
from the ever increasing
slipperiness of the slope
I was now on, heading toward
parental shaking of heads
and the shameful label of
'bitter disappointment'
which is the last thing in the world
I would ever want to be
because that would mean
I had failed.

The Summer of '67

We were looking for love
I think, that week,
the four of us, single
in the summer of '67.

The Roker Hotel,
steps crumbling,
white-washed walls
pitted with weariness
of the defeated,
but we didn't care.

Cross-legged on bar stools,
cigarette in one hand
(for sex appeal),
Snowball with cherry
in the other, we listened
dreamily while the
Dansette in the corner
boasting a hold of
eight singles at once,
sang to us all night,

and as we promised
over and over
to wear flowers in
our hair if we went to
San Francisco,
we bathed passionately

in alcoholic daze
and smoky haze
as we looked for love.

Our Mother

berated herself constantly,
scrunched herself up time
after laboured time like
another useless draft,
yet poured herself seamlessly
into beautiful floral art,
sweeping statements of
Hogarth curve,
studies in driftwood, bulrush
and sweet grass reeds.
We glimpsed the essence of
who she was.

Years later, after she had gone
we discovered brush strokes
of a girl who was only fourteen;
a church by moonlight,
roseate apples on rustic table
and sailboats at peace
on a halcyon sea.
If only she could have
sailed those calm waters,
if only she could have seen
what we could see,
if only she could have
loved herself -
just a little.

Elephant Trousers

It seems that summer has given up,
gloomy, overweight clouds
sagging, grey-bellied,
although a salvaged remnant of
watery blue breaks through,
like the fabric you bought for my dress;
I'd had my eye on it for weeks,
faded, outstayed welcome in
shop window, scrap-box demoted.
Nice and cheap though
and you had enough
broderie anglaise trimming at home
to brighten it up.

Out came the Singer;
how I loved that machine,
its treadle and spools, smell of oil
and complicated attachments,
your stoical fast pedalling,
full of purpose.
You showed me how to use it,
delicate threads of patience
stitched into every pin-pricked lesson,
with yards and yards of laughing love.
I can see you now
looking up at today's clouds.

There isn't enough blue sky up there
to sew an elephant a pair of trousers.

Mothering

She was like a velvet blanket
with a gift to turn
childhood ailments into fun;
magazine specials,
puzzle books
favourite food.

She was the one to turn to
when life dealt a losing hand.
And she was the one whose
tears meant most when
my firstborn emerged,
her gift as much as mine.

Then one day she forgot my name.
Her brain skipped a beat.
She looked at me,
her gaze more eloquent than words.

Are you my sister?
quizzical, childlike,
as she sipped her tea.

One-Way Ticket

We were waiting for the bus.
You should be wearing a hat
she said,
you'll catch your death.

I'd spotted her strolling down the
street, window shopping,
chatting to a stranger,
timeworn gabardine navigating
her frailty, brown fuzzy beret,
not so much Basque as
church bring and buy,
clutching a bag that matched nothing,
tight, like a security blanket,
contents stoically protecting her past;
Stratton compact, sweet pressed nostalgia,
bright red lipstick, barely worn,
as garish as she never was,
and Yardley 4711 eau de cologne
with its little red rubber stopper,
to be dabbed sparingly, of course,
middle finger only.
Oh, and a piece of coal should she come
across someone about to take an exam.
My daughter was in the legal profession,
she told the stranger.
I was a secretary, mum.
Same thing, she said.
She told me she still had a bus ticket

somewhere from the days of
Samuel Ledgard.
Now they were real buses, she said
Anyway, where are we going now?
she asked, excited as a child.
I smiled and gently took her arm.
Home, I said.

To Remember You

I'm here because it's the dutiful thing
in the eyes of family and friends,
but this isn't about them.
This isn't where you are
and when I'm away from here
I see you doing things you used to do;
I hear your laughter and feel your love,
watch your expertise with floral art
and cake decoration
so natural to you.
I smile when I hear you say you have no talent.
I don't need the headstone, names and dates
or the faded flowers in a graveyard,
to remember you.

Caesarean Section

Saturday, 30 September 1972

Sunlight edged through bevelled glass,
hovered softly over water on
bedside table,
a jug of liquid gold

waiting for painful sips to be
taken as surges rose and fell.
You had decided it was time;
we would do this together.

You shifted and shifted
hour after laboured hour;
I pushed – in vain – until
suddenly, it seemed, all my
senses were cancelled out,
crossed off the list of essentials
for giving birth.

I clawed my way out of anaesthesia,
a drug-riddled fog; there was
no doctor, no nurse, no family –

No baby.

Twenty eight life-long hours later,
wheels trundling through endless
corridors to nowhere

led me slowly towards you;
stone-faced uniform and
a hostile silence;
this extra work had broken routine.

We finally met, still painfully
divided by unyielding glass
but you were there;
you were so beautiful –
vulnerable, innocent,
impossible and real.

And I had failed you already.

Mirror

Bevelled edge of leafy flowers and vines
a keepsake that I hang upon my wall.
This mirror that I see before me shines;
it seems the years were minutes after all.
Sweetest face you are never far from me,
memories like a favourite food each day
and in my heart I know I'll ever see
the way you always helped me find my way.
And now that time has passed and you are gone
I see a person looking back at me;
she's older, wiser and a little drawn
and though I know it's me who I can see
you're looking back and smiling at the grey
and in this glass it's you I see each day.

Birthday Meal

I sit next to him,
browse photos taken
across the table;
bemoan process of
ageing upon skin.
Mum, he says,
You have a forty-year-old son
with a receding hairline;
you can't still expect
to look twenty.
But I do.

At the Hairdresser's

I look in the mirror,
head like Tin Man,
ask myself,
Why do I do it –
why not just grow
old gracefully?
I ignore the reply,

immerse myself instead
in *Hello* magazine;
Victoria Beckham's two-year-old
sporting designer clothes,
minor celeb from somewhere,
nowhere, Gucci heels,
Balenciaga bag,
sprawled outrageously over
a leather sofa to die for, and
the poshest of posh celebrity
weddings and all its
tacky trappings; until

Ping!

I am done, cooked to
perfection, all set to re-emerge
into an altogether more
sophisticated, intellectual world,
and ready to resume my justified criticism
of people who doll themselves up
and read trash.

God's Wonderful World

He called it God's wonderful world.
It was the richest ingredient
in his blood and he loved
everything that came with it.
Shared tales of his ships,
Ullapool and Weirpol,
stories of the albatross,
revered feathered giants
motionless for hours,
hovering souls, he said, of sailors
swallowed by the greedy sea.
And huge scavenging vultures,
a gloomy black mass above the ship,
waiting.
He worked below deck too,
in stifling greasy engine rooms,
braved storms I could never imagine,
escaped the imminent call of death twice,
and spent months on end away
from home.
I don't believe he was truly happy
anywhere else.

Smiling at Death

Your whole life was wrapped around you
on that day,
propped up on a pillowy white cloud,
a few extra ones, cool and crisp
arranged in a special way,
a privilege for the dying.

How could your tiny fragile frame
have carried so much,
braved storms at sea,
ministered prayers from pulpit.
And all those swimming lessons
you gave me;
you had the patience of Job.
And the turnip faces you carved
for Halloween, they were perfect;
(you would have cringed at pumpkins).
But then you could do everything;
you knew everything too.
You tried to show me
how to use a slide rule;
I still haven't a clue.

And there,
on a warm day, early May
in a special bed for the dying
lay all of that,
your whole life in a cradle of time,
and it weighed next to nothing –

except for your smile.
Your smile was stronger than ever,
big enough to carry us all
as it led you, without doubt,
to a place you had always believed in
and where you were sure
we would meet again.

You turned your head toward me.
Is my grandma here yet? you asked
in whispered voice.
Now it was my turn to smile.
I looked into your bright but fading eyes.
Yes, dad, I said, *I think she is.*
And you slipped away,
smiling at death

Transposition

I could see through the wood and brass.

A seafaring man fighting for country,
raising three children, ministering prayers.
I search persistently for this lost life,
its fullness, its vibrancy.

Maybe it's in the strange flower
I found in the garden,
the one I know I didn't plant,
or in the poem that writes itself
seamlessly, despite me.

Life not extinguished, transposed.

Suitcase

This old case is so full of us all
it will hardly close;
I feel the need to sit on it
to keep us safely packed in.

I think it was the only one we owned;
it took the whole family to
Bridlington and back every year.
When the 3-IN-ONE came out
I knew the sea wasn't far away.
Just a touch to lubricate the catches.
You said they seized up over the years
a bit like you.
I can see laughter lines at the
corners of your eyes;
you were the strongest part of us
and as long as you were there
everything would be all right.

But when I open the lid now
I can smell hardship and fear
dwelling beneath the brittle,
yellow pages of newspaper that
line its thick cardboard base.
I know only too well that
this courageous, time-worn handle
has been gripped
determinedly many times
taking you to places far from the

safety of the seafront and the
fusty rooms of the small hotel
where, at our mother's request,
Henry and Roy would
fry yesterday's potatoes for breakfast.

Baby Haiku

Tiny seed planted
germination soon in place
fruit of the autumn.

Toddlers wait with joy
Baby three is on its way
Six feet pattering.

I'm the One

You look at me
across the room,
smile, eyes intense,
a look that says
I'm the one,
walk eagerly
towards me.

Arms clasped tight
around my neck,
head resting
in its curve –
your favourite place –
you kiss my cheek.

Twenty months old,
brimming with love.

What It Is

It's not called a Something Interceptor,
It's called a Jedi Interceptor!
He laughs,
shaking his five-year-old head
at my bewilderment.

Whatever its name
it was the reason
we sat together on the sofa
for the whole weekend
apart from trips out here and there.
I was given the privileged position
of Light Saber Holder,
a duty carried out with care.
I learned how R2D2 was built,
how Anakin once fell into lava
and lost all his hair
(thankfully not forever).

But what I learned most
was how the love of a child
is set apart from any other,
its unconditional quality,
its gritty honesty,
its patience.

This is Holiday

Wearing tee shirt, shorts and
sandals, your face reflects
contented joy as you kick debris
on the forest floor;
dust of ages forms puffs of memory
and you feel no need to complain
about the grit stuck to your feet.

You look up in awe,
ponder the impossible tallness
of trees and spot a red squirrel
flit past, amazed it isn't grey,
collect dead sticks for your
treasure box, and pine cones;
mum helps to choose the best
to hold glitter for Christmas,
a concept too much to conceive
on a day such as this.

And as the long, tired day begins
to yawn, you, wrapped cosily
in a soft, fluffy towel
snuggle close and whisper in my ear,
This is holiday.

Awestruck

He stands alone
clasping precious finds.
Around him, slender
guardians point high
toward winter sky;
look down as tiny feet
kick discarded leaves.
So much to learn,
so much wonder,
so much time.

For Theodore, aged 3

How you made me laugh today
when you brought out a train
to put in a car park we had made
on the garden seats
and how I made you laugh
when one of my cars rolled off
into the hole where the
garden umbrella will sit
when summer arrives.
How your eyes met mine
and in that moment
you taught me
that these are the treasured things
and all the other stuff doesn't matter
because love is the key
and yours pours out
like a gushing waterfall
a glistening bright sparkly one
that flows and flows and
never stops at all.

Innocence

I sit beside you stroking your hair,
feel the pureness in every wispy strand.
You tell me your nose is running;
I wipe it with a tissue and
we carry on reading the book.
You giggle because
Mr Magnolia wears only one boot,
has an old trumpet that goes tooty toot.
My hand brushes your cheek as I turn the page;
you smile, snuggle closer.
I hope you can keep at least a small slice of this;
I hope the world treats you well.

Solomon's Light

Who cares
about avoiding cliché?
Your presence is like
a magic patch of sunshine
on grey November days.
When your smile
peeps round the door
there is a bright light and
my fears know that for now
they are beaten;
you are the breath of fresh air
that I crave.
And today
when you toddled
full length of the room,
successfully for the first time,
bearing a gift especially for me –
two stickle bricks in a pan –
I knew that this was the start
of something big.

Song of Life

He sings, constantly –
Van Morrison, The Beatles,
Neil Young, James Taylor,
Paul Simon; even
Ella Fitzgerald and Ray Charles
swing by occasionally.
Then there are the hymns;
never gets the words right.
That's not the point, he tells her.

He sings arguments too.
Sometimes she could hit him.
Then she hears him singing to
his grandchildren,
stops in her tracks,
and ponders on how life would be
if he weren't here.

Part Three
Drowning

Daughter

She sat reluctantly at the piano,
could have been very good
If she'd kept it up,
but being thirteen got in the way.
My friend had called and
we sat drinking vodka.
She burned a hole in the sofa,
and we laughed.

Angels, by Robbie Williams;
she played beautifully,
even my booze-soaked head
could hear that much.
We sat drinking and
crying with the music,
and she played dutifully, beautifully,
again and again and again.

And then I told her I was
taking my friend home
to help her bath her two small children
because *she* was too drunk to do it.

And I left her at home, alone.

Phoebe and Me

As you nestle cosily,
your contented purr
vibrating on my lap,
I recall the day I brought you home.

I had driven, over the alcohol limit,
to visit a friend after her desperate
call for help; we were two of a kind,
both lost in a hostile, foreign land.

I found her lying in bed
surrounded by a swarm of
newborn kittens.

You stumbled over to me
small and vulnerable,
eyes like fallen stars.
I held you in one cupped hand,
and, drunk, fell in love.

Twelve and a half years sober
and I am still in love with you.

My friend died.

Surrender

I became a street
actor on stilts
to see over
walls erected by
years of despair.

I would strut clumsily,
attempting to dance to
whoever played
the loudest tune,
juggle frantically
with balls of
denial, resentment,
guilt, and fear, until

quite unexpectedly,
the stilts cracked
and forced me
to the ground.

I knew the journey
had begun and I thanked God
that the performance
was finally over.

Painting the Future

In the treatment centre for alcoholism,
attendance at art therapy
was 'suggested'.
I was arrogant and stubborn.
*I want to stop drinking,
not draw stupid pictures.*

Today, I found my artwork,
like a drawing by a child.
And that is what I was,
a bewildered infant, lost,
fearful and alone,
my arrogance a mere defence.

A long winding road,
dark, threat-laden sky,
and far in the impossible future
a clump of yellow primroses
in the sun:
a bright yellow circle
in the top right-hand corner.

Today I am standing next to the flowers
and the sun is real.

On the 10th anniversary of my recovery from alcoholism.

Sobriety – Ten Years On

Ten years on I still hate parties.
Lucid conversation dissolves
into embarrassing gibberish,
as I recoil from alcohol-drenched
kisses, and ten years on
I can still sit in self-righteous judgement
of people simply trying
to enjoy themselves.

But alcohol dragged me swiftly
beyond the realms of enjoyment
to a lonely space of despair;
it lured me toward dark, desolate,
dangerous places,
stole my dignity and self-worth, almost
robbed me of family and friends,
and nearly killed me.

Ten years on, I would not
trade my sobriety for anything.

Part Four
Dancing in the Rain

MRI Scan

She asks what music
I would like to listen to;
I suggest Vivaldi.
Confident nod of approval,
I can be accommodated.
Then she asks if I am okay.
I tell her I'm fine;
What else can I say?
Besides, does she really want
to know?
She has a list to get through.

The bed glides mournfully along,
reluctant coffin into the unknown.
I grip the panic button, but not
too tight so it bleeps;
I want this to be over.
I wasn't aware that Vivaldi had
composed The *1812 Overture*;
can't hear it much anyway,
gruesome noises magnetically
resonating images of
inflammatory changes playing
games with my brain.
I try to think of pleasant things
but draw a blank,
so I decide to smile instead;
it works.

The return journey begins,
slow, but less mournful.
I haven't been cremated after all
and amazingly, the sea-sick green
walls look exquisitely appealing.

I could never be a potholer.

Lost in the Post

It's seven thirty; they've started early,
churning political expertise in a rusty
cement mixer till it is smooth, creamy
and set into a new south-faced existence.

Weary face in a tired van pulls up,
pours calcium into brittle bones of daily
life, his own rattled by plastic progress;
business is dead.

Lone jogger pads her daily ritual to
crescendo as a brisk breeze edges
its sharpness through my open window.

And here comes Boy Racer, dead on cue,
screeches to a tedious halt,
picks up his friend in the white shirt
with no tie.
They say he's the clever one, Boy Racer,
can park his car on a postage stamp

which makes me think about my life and
how it seems all of it fits onto a
stamp these days,
a small, watery blue one,
second class,
lost in the post.

What It's About

It wasn't really about
floor wipes;
she just bought the
wrong ones, that's all,
it didn't matter,
but that's where
the argument began.

What it was truly about
was my immobility,
my lack of control,
their helplessness.
I know I am not the
only one who suffers.

Tomorrow the shop
will open again and
we will buy the correct
floor wipes, the ones
that fit on my special mop.

A Bad Good Dream

Eyes half open
you realise it's morning
and although a dream-soaked
forest of night with a
star-scattered moon track,
insisted everything was well
and as before –
so excited you found you could run,
right arm strong again
pointing full stretch toward a snowy owl –
daylight now smirks a different truth.
You slide from the bed,
good side first.

The mirror sees it all;
a tsunami in a single tear.

The Party's Over

The Halloween party was a joy
but it's over and now
I feel left behind.
Family and friends have gone
wearing their independence
like casual accessories
slung over shoulders.

I look at the creased-up smile
on a tired pumpkin-faced balloon
as it lies limp on the floor.
I too feel limp,
haven't the energy to pick it up
or do anything else at all and
writing or reading, which usually
keeps me feeling alive,
just isn't enough.

I simply want what I cannot have.

Teacher

You wander in and out
so slowly now,
a painful limp,
a hip joint not quite what it was.
But your needs are few;
a warm spot on the sofa,
the promise of occasional fish,
a small patch outside
for private stuff and
a spoonful of fresh air –
your entire world
on the space of a stamp.

And yet you waddle quite happily back in,
settle yourself on my knee
a purring engine ticking over,
dribbling pleasure,
closing bliss-drenched eyes
as I stroke your chin.
We remember Christmas
how you played with a fallen bauble,
scored an invisible goal and
looked at me as if to say,
I've still got it!

Do you crave anything at all?
Your gone life? The lost wild?
I don't think so.

I could learn much from you.

Real

Cry your heart out if you need to,
rail against the world and
all its seeming unfairness,
because acceptance isn't a pretty gift
tied with pastel ribbon bows;
it's a trundling wagon making its
way clumsily over rough terrain,
and you may often

lose your grip, fall off in the
desert sand, find yourself on
all fours in a bad dream
trying to catch up, cling on,
feet dragging in flying dust,
helpless and hopeless.

What I'm trying to say is
keep going, keep clinging,
reach out and don't ever give up,
but allow your sorrow
its rightful place;
let it be.
It is real.

Incredulous

Sometimes I laugh out loud,
Incredulous.

How I can no longer fold
towels corner to corner,
stack them, folds to the front
colour coded.
How sheets slip resolute like
liquid silk through erring
fingers, as I try to grip,
land defeated at baffled feet;
how I can't spread jam on
toast, tie bows, cut food,
fasten belts, buttons, or
sign my name.
It's all so ludicrous, and

Sometimes I sob out loud,
Incredulous.

Trapped

This morning
acceptance just flew away
accompanied by two magpies
as they took off over gardens
into distant fields
now green again and able to breathe
after welcome thaw.
I opened the door,
saw the grass and sensed a
sharp-edged wind
brush against a pale
complaisant sun.
And I wanted to run.

Shoes

They sit, redundant
on the wardrobe floor;
strappy sandals, flip-flops,
high heels, the gold strapless
I wore for our son's wedding
and those with delicate
butterflies for a dinner
dance where Ronan Keating
was guest singer.
(I could have taken him home.)

Then those less redundant,
flat lace-ups in full view,
lined up on the bedroom floor,
just in case;
Velcro mocking in triumph.

Today I gave them all to the
lady who cleans for me;
she's going to look, maybe keep
a pair, and take the rest to Oxfam.

I feel like a part of me has died.

What I Thought Was Mine

Today as I walk
toward hope of a clearer truth,
the one that all the books say is the best,
I will still rail against this pernicious disease
and go nowhere gently
because I am who I am.
I shall do mindful moments and meditate,
emerge feeling free –
for a while at least
assured that this is the way
because we all know that
now is all we have.
But beneath all,
I will silently seethe and shout
while I pointlessly crave my old life
as every day that passes it seems
a little more of what I thought was mine
is taken away.

Dancing in the Dark

In my mind I am still

Dancing in the Dark,

those kind moonlit hours

that allow me to feel

like me again,

till daylight beckons and

I leave him to his Glory Days

and he leaves me to mine,

and they can be glorious

if I let them.

And I will dance again tonight

in my dreams, in the dark.

Someone told me there will be a new moon.

This poem is special to me as it marks a personal turning point. I had previously refused to use a wheelchair to my own detriment as it meant I couldn't go to certain places. But my desire to see Bruce Springsteen in concert outweighed my reluctance and so I hired a chair and had the most amazing evening. I have used one a few times since, although it's my least favourite mode of transport; acceptance is ongoing!

Wilmer

It was definitely on its last wheels,
heavily weighed down with ghost scars,
years of invisible struggles piled,
precarious, on an old sagging seat.
If I hadn't been so heavily reliant,
I would have jumped off and
helped it into the lift.
Then a waitress on the ferry
knocked it as she passed.
It quivered like a frightened dog
and I felt sad.
A strange feeling of empathy
washed over me and I reached out
and touched it, gave it a name.
I told Wilmer not to fret and said
this time she could travel light.
There would be no scars left by me;
this was going to be a good trip.

Accepting Acceptance

Don't get me wrong,
I love writing;
it has kept me alive for
the past three years,
every word a stitch
in the coloured lining of
chronic disease

But if I could choose and
could walk again, out of the door
with my beautiful dog, Jack
I would quite happily
never write another word.

Acceptance is a trek,
a journey without end;
there may be stop-off points
along the way, places to reflect,
enjoy a well-earned view
but don't expect to arrive for the last time,
to be able to say,
Ah, at last I'm here, it's done
because it never is.

My Body

Sometimes I want to
leap out of my body,
leave it, discard it,
I feel it has let me down.

But it's not to blame;
it houses me, embraces me,
nourishes the best it can
despite a raging war.
I need to treat it with
respect,
compassion,
love.

I stroke my arm gently as
if it were a cat nestled in
the warm bowl of my lap.

Caramelised Hazelnut Praline

I won't give up,
I won't give in,
I will not let it beat me.
It's persistent for sure,
cruel and sneaky.
It watches, waits,
and just when you think
you are steady again,
it gives you a mean, sharp
flick, and over you go,
a teetering pin to
complete the strike.
But it won't win,
I won't let it, because,
you see, I have too much
to do, too many things
to see, and so much new
chocolate to try.

I think I will start with
caramelised hazelnut praline.

Neutral

It may say something

about me, the way I am;

I always resort

to brown and cream.

Maybe there is an

underlying fear of change,

the need to blend in,

go unnoticed, hide.

Or maybe I just like

cream and brown.

But change is good;

I will buy a new cushion.

It's Okay

It's okay, I say quietly,
it's only a plastic bag.
But he isn't convinced,
goes to his bed.
Then I bring out the Hoover;
he rushes into the back room.
I massage his silky head
as he escapes into sleep,
whimpers his way to a safer place
until the fireworks begin and
he is at my feet all a-quiver.
I tell him I understand the firework thing;
they make me nervous too.
I gently lift his ear, whisper,
(so the cats can't hear)

I do understand you know,
how frightening life can be,
about courage, and how
it isn't the absence of fear
but being brave enough to
walk through it anyway.
You are doing just fine.

A Dog's Perspective

She's coming downstairs.
I can hear her moans and groans,
predict her first words,

*Now then Jacky, my lovely boy,
how are you?
Life's a bugger isn't it?*

I sit dutifully as she proffers
my morning chew.
(Why she pauses to choose
a colour is beyond me.)
I take it outside, start my day.

She doesn't moan much really,
though she can go on.
I don't mind, and when I lay
my head gently on her knee,
lick her smooth hand and gaze
adoringly into her eyes
I really do mean it.

Besides, I know there are biscuits.

Please Don't Cry

Oh, please don't cry,
they sometimes say,
though I think it's
their discomfort.

But it's okay to cry;
it untangles threads of feeling,
sorts them into length, colour,
texture and weight,
so the embroidery can begin again
under new light.

Truth

Sitting outside, sipping the
realness of hot chocolate with
hazelnut syrup and sprinkles,
I realise I have become
divorced from my reality,
stubbornly resisting my own
exigent cries for help.

What does that say about me?
Arrogant, too proud to
graciously receive simple
acts of kindness,
perched on a pedestal
above humanness.
These are not assets.

Illness has exuded valuable clues;
I could learn something.
So I continue to kiss the
whispery froth, and allow it to
dissolve slowly into contrarious
lips toward a softer,
quieter, much clearer truth.

Letting Go of the Knife

I chose the wrong food,
Aubergine Involtini,
large slices, tough skin;
should have gone for curry.
I picked a piece up but a
large dollop of 'hot' splashed
my face, dropped like a
dead wet fish back on the plate.

She looked at me; I nodded,
passed her the plate.
She sliced the food gently,
not willy-nilly like cutting a child's food
at a busy meal, but lovingly, kindly
into neat bite-sized pieces
of tenderness.

There are many walls out there;
I walked round one tonight.

Coming in from the Cold

I have decided to let it in,
MS that is.
I have made it stand out there
in all weathers, biting cold,
hail, strong winds and snow,
but it looks at me through the
window, stubbornly determined.

So I open the door, invite it
to sit down.
We chat about this and that
and I make us both coffee.
I smile with conviction and say
that as long as it understands
I am in charge,
we will get along just fine.

Falling Skyward

Silver spines of hoar frost
cover the unsuspecting garden
in a web of lace,
a rare sight this winter.
It shouts for attention,
to be captured in a moment,
recorded forever.

But the world
has turned sideways,
plant pots at eye level,
empty snail house,
opted for warmer
climes perhaps,
hairy spider
raising his hat –
too close for comfort.

Falling can be helpful,
makes you pause, see,
connect.

I drag myself up,
dignity restored,

and amid
startled blue air,
click the shutter.

Dancing in the Rain

And the dance began that day
when doctors frowned
as they gave me the news,
when poetry jumped from
a silent place,
running around
like a frantic dog
chasing its tail.
When dark clouds ripped open
their grey-bellied seams,
and showered my fears
with hope
as I danced my way home
in the rain
towards faith.

If It Works

If prayer works, pray,

someone once said

so I try;

it doesn't come easy.

Sometimes in desperation,

(and I wouldn't tell everyone this),

I even kiss the sky,

hopes of a fanfare,

cherubim and seraphim

leading the way with flaming swords

down elusive paths.

But mostly I contemplate quietly,

feel a gentle flame of gratitude

for the good in people,

and their love becomes my strength.

Fear

Today I shake hands with you,
say, *Good morning, how are you?*
We sit together on a bench
in the light of a fresh day.
I breathe new breath,
smile with awareness,
become comfortable,
feel as one.
A sense of calm arrives
from somewhere, nowhere,
wraps me in certain trust
and the soft whisper of
Yes, it's okay, you can go now.

Still

You don't have to
keep moving
if you don't know
which way to turn.
It's okay to stand
still for a while.

Morning Prayer

The house feels quiet first thing,
lonely even.
I let the cat in and you waft past.
You are persistent for sure.

But it's no good, it won't work,
we're not meant to be.
You need someone who welcomes,
someone who is sure, and I'm not;
we're not compatible.

I resume my morning ritual,
fresh morning tea,
muddled thoughts stirred.
But I can't quite escape the tiny
hint of light in the far corner
of my eye.

Give me a try,
no strings —
just for today.

Now

Life changed and
suddenly it seemed
I had stalled
quite out of the blue
in the middle of a busy road
traffic all around me
this way and that,
impatient, hurried
and a cloud of sadness
overwhelmed me,
total eclipse

until I realised where I was;
it was simple, I was right here
in the now
where clouds will never
look the same again
and with all the time I wanted
just to be;
freedom and a second chance
to notice all I had missed.

Author's note: This was written at a breakthrough moment while I was having a bad MS attack in 2012 in the form of optic neuritis which involved some loss of my sight. Simultaneously, my daughter was doing research for her MA and came across a book called How to be Sick *by Toni Bernhard. If not for this book, I have no idea where I would be now. It inspired this poem which has become very important to me.*

All This

Alone in the house this morning,
except for two cats and a dog
basking in behind-the-window January sun;
they could be meditating.

Leaf shadows of the eucalyptus
quiver on the wall
like bewildered butterflies
and the patio door is ajar.
A feathered chorus floats into the room,
a melodic liquid song.
The kettle boils.

There is something extraordinary
in these ordinary things
and I am happy;
I have learned to love silence.
I feel I could sit here for hours
just watching the measured breathing
of two cats and a dog,
listening to the sound of
hope filling an open window,
and sipping tea
All this,
and then soon, the edge of spring
like the edge of youth,
where everything is about to become,
and nothing is yet past.

Don't Let Go

The more you lose,
the more you find
to hold onto.

Grab it with a sure,
tight fist and
don't let go.

Be Awake

Be Awake

When you walk along the path
do not be unaware of how
your legs are moving,
how your hands are free,
or oblivious to the tender
wilderness that bends and sways
but never breaks
and don't just hear but listen
to the comforting call
of a collared dove as he
tips his hat to say hello
though some may say he
only squawks and swears.
And the wood pigeons too,
listen to them.

I'm not saying stop being busy
because that's on
the to-do list of life.
All I am saying is
be aware,
don't sleep through it all,
don't miss anything;
be awake

Bennison Books

Bennison Books has four imprints:

Contemporary Classics
Great writing from new authors

Non-Fiction
Interesting and useful works written by experts

People's Classics
Handpicked golden oldies by favourite and forgotten authors

Poetic Licence
Poetry and prosetry

Bennison Books is named after Ronald Bennison, an aptly named blessing.

Bennisonbooks.com

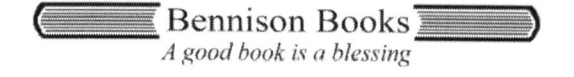

Bennison Books
A good book is a blessing

Printed in Great Britain
by Amazon